First World War
and Army of Occupation
War Diary
France, Belgium and Germany

20 DIVISION
59 Infantry Brigade
Cameronians (Scottish Rifles)
2nd Battalion
1 February 1918 - 8 April 1919

WO95/2117/2

The Naval & Military Press Ltd
www.nmarchive.com
Published in association with The National Archives

Published by

The Naval & Military Press Ltd

Unit 10 Ridgewood Industrial Park,

Uckfield, East Sussex,

TN22 5QE England

Tel: +44 (0) 1825 749494

www.naval-military-press.com

www.nmarchive.com

This diary has been reprinted in facsimile from the original. Any imperfections are inevitably reproduced and the quality may fall short of modern type and cartographic standards.

© Crown Copyright
Images reproduced by permission of The National Archives, London, England, 2015.

Contents

Document type	Place/Title	Date From	Date To
Heading	WO95/2117 20 Division 59 Infantry Brigade 2 Battalion Cameronians (Scottish Rifles) Feb 1918-April 1919		
Heading	20th Division 59th Infy Bde 2nd Bn Cameronians (Scottish Rifles) Feb 1918-Apr 1919 From 8 Div 23 Bde		
Miscellaneous	2nd Bn Scottish Rifles Photographs 3.		
Diagram etc			
Miscellaneous	No. 3 Carte Postale		
Miscellaneous			
Miscellaneous	Lieut A.C. Marshall R.A.S.C. 20th Division	17/06/1919	17/06/1919
Miscellaneous	With 23rd Brigade. 8th Division		
Miscellaneous	With 59th Brigade, 20th Division		
Miscellaneous	30245 Pte. James Towers 2/Scottish Rifles		
Heading	59th Brigade 20th Division. 2nd Battalion The Scottish Rifles February 1918 Apr 19		
War Diary		01/02/1918	17/02/1918
Heading	59th Brigade. 20th Division. 2nd Battalion The Scottish Rifles March 1918		
War Diary	Chaulnes	01/03/1918	21/03/1918
War Diary	Beauvois	22/03/1918	22/03/1918
War Diary	Voyennes	23/03/1918	24/03/1918
War Diary	Nesle	25/03/1918	25/03/1918
War Diary	Quenelles	26/03/1918	26/03/1918
War Diary	Folie	27/03/1918	31/03/1918
Miscellaneous	Herewith War Diary For Month of April 1918	07/05/1918	07/05/1918
War Diary	Domart	01/04/1918	01/04/1918
War Diary	Quevauvillers	02/04/1918	03/04/1918
War Diary	Aumont	04/04/1918	09/04/1918
War Diary	Rambures	10/04/1918	10/04/1918
War Diary	Dargnies	11/04/1918	18/04/1918
War Diary	Berles Monchy	19/04/1918	28/04/1918
War Diary	Berles Between Arras & St. Pol On Main Arras Road (Lens Sheet)	29/04/1918	30/04/1918
Miscellaneous	Headquarters 20th Division	02/06/1918	02/06/1918
War Diary	Berles	01/05/1918	16/05/1918
War Diary	Lens Sector	17/05/1918	31/05/1918
Operation(al) Order(s)	2nd Bn Scottish Rifles Order No. 5	02/05/1918	02/05/1918
Miscellaneous	2nd Bn. Scottish Rifles Order No. 12 By Lieut Colonel V. C. Sandelands D.S.O. Commanding	27/05/1918	27/05/1918
War Diary		01/06/1918	31/07/1918
War Diary	Lorette Camp.	01/08/1918	31/08/1918
War Diary	Trenches Avion Section Left Bn.	01/09/1918	13/09/1918
War Diary	Line	14/09/1918	06/10/1918
War Diary	Berles	07/10/1918	30/10/1918
War Diary	Cambrai	30/10/1918	02/11/1918
War Diary	Cauroir	03/11/1918	04/11/1918
War Diary	St Aubert	05/11/1918	06/11/1918
War Diary	Sommaing	07/11/1918	08/11/1918
War Diary	Jenlain	09/11/1918	10/11/1918

War Diary	St. Waast	11/11/1918	11/11/1918
War Diary	Taisnieres	12/11/1918	22/11/1918
War Diary	Wargnies Le-Petit	23/11/1918	23/11/1918
War Diary	Bermerain-St-Martin	24/11/1918	24/11/1918
War Diary	St Vaast	25/11/1918	26/11/1918
War Diary	Cambrai	27/11/1918	29/11/1918
War Diary	Toutencourt	30/11/1918	30/11/1918
War Diary	Toutencourt Ref. Map. Lens. 1/100,000	01/12/1918	08/12/1918
War Diary	Toutencourt	09/12/1918	31/01/1919
Miscellaneous	Headquarters, 20th Division	03/03/1919	03/03/1919
War Diary	Toutencourt	01/02/1919	19/02/1919
War Diary	Raincheval	18/02/1919	28/02/1919
Miscellaneous	D.A.G. 3rd Echelon	03/04/1919	03/04/1919
War Diary	Raincheval	01/03/1919	08/03/1919
War Diary	Terramesnil	10/03/1919	30/03/1919
War Diary	Havre	31/03/1919	31/03/1919
Miscellaneous	D.A.G., 3rd Echelon France	09/04/1919	09/04/1919
War Diary	Havre	01/04/1919	08/04/1919

WO 95/2117

20 Division
59 Infantry Brigade
2 Battalion Cameronians (Scottish Rifles)

Feb 1918 — April 1919

(2)

CAMERONIANS
2ND BN (SCOTTISH RIFLES)
FEB 1918 – APR 1919

from 8 BN 23 BDE

20TH DIVISION
59TH INFY BDE

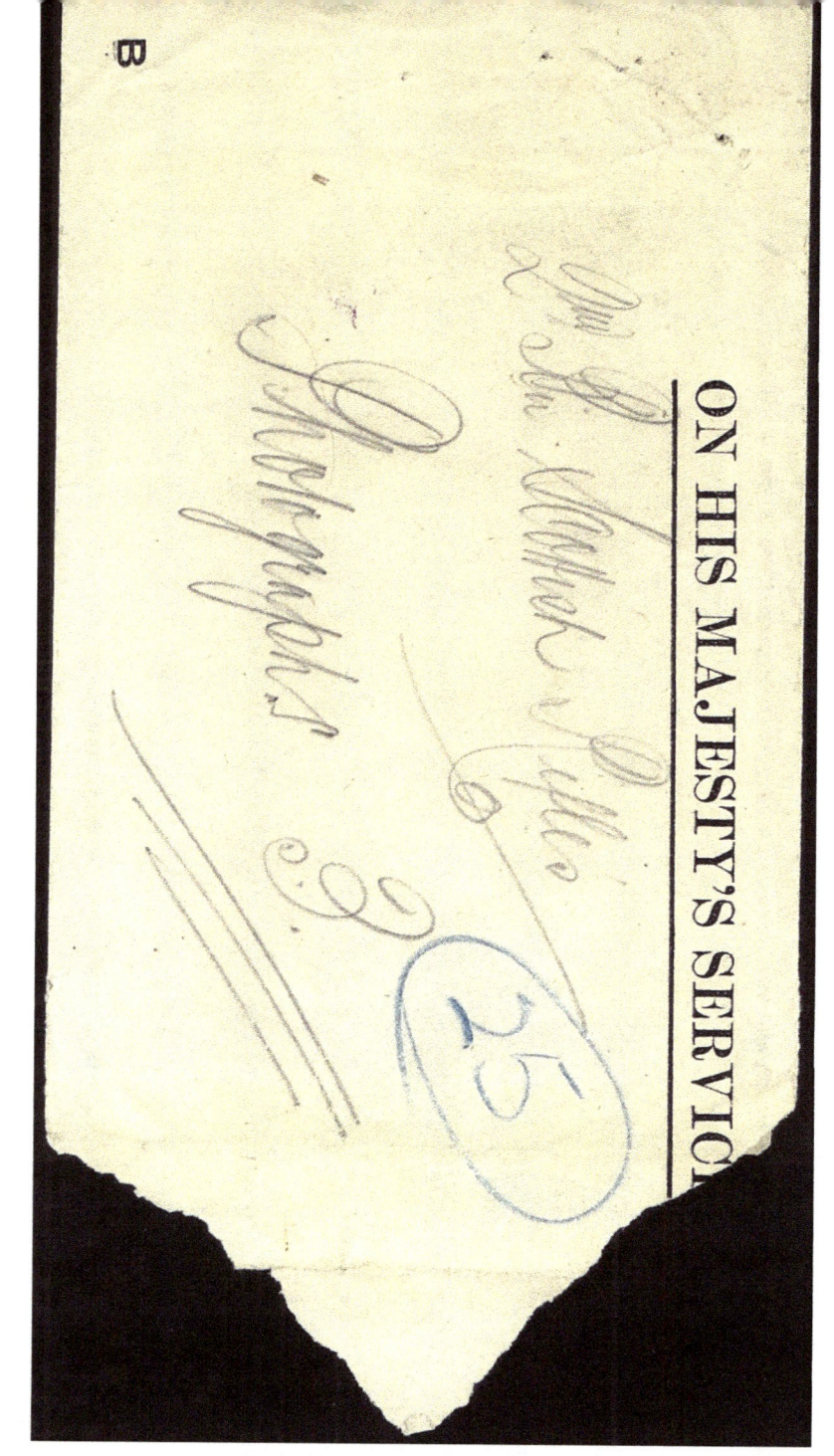

ON HIS MAJESTY'S SERVICE

Dr G Arthur Pollo
Photographs
25

CARTE POSTALE

Bn., A.I.F. (Preston).

No. 30245 Pte. James Towers, 2nd Bn. Sco. Rif.

For most conspicuous bravery and devotion to duty at Mericourt on October 6, 1918, under heavy fire, five runners having failed to deliver an important message, Pte. Towers, well aware of the fate of the runners who had already attempted the task, volunteered for the duty.

In spite of heavy fire opened on him as soon as he moved, he went straight through from cover to cover and eventually delivered the message.

His valour, determination, and utter disregard of danger were an inspiring example to all.

No. 43839 Pte. Alfred Wilkinson, 1/5th Bn., Manch. R. (T.F.) (Leigh).

For most conspicuous bravery and devotion to duty on October 20, 1918, during the attack on Marou, when, four runners in succession having been killed in an endeavour to deliver a message to the supporting company, Pte. Wilkinson volunteered for the duty. He succeeded in delivering the message, though the journey involved exposure to extremely heavy machine-gun and shell fire for 600 yards. He showed magnificent courage and complete indifference to danger, thinking only of the needs of his company and entirely disregarding any consideration for personal safety.

Throughout the remainder of the day Pte. Wilkinson continued to do splendid work.

No. 3102 Pte. Thomas Ricketts, 1st Bn. R. Newfoundland R.

For most conspicuous bravery and devotion to duty on October 14, 1918, during the advance

(Continued at foot of next column.)

THE ARMY AND THE LIFE-BOAT SERVICE.

THE HONOURED MEMORY OF THE GALLANT DEAD.

At the present moment Standing Committees of the glorious regiments of the British Army have under consideration

THE BEST FORM OF MEMORIAL

to the Officers and Men, who have given their lives for King and Country, and have added fresh laurels to the honour of the Regiment.

It would be difficult to find a Memorial better fitted to commemorate the noble dead than

A LIFE-BOAT

endowed in perpetuity. For a Life-boat is a living instrument for the saving of valuable lives; it is the very embodiment of heroism and humanity in action; and the achievements of the Life-boat Crews have been linked, throughout this terrible struggle, with the fortunes of Britain and her Allies; and with the rescue of thousands of gallant men, who have been restored to their home and enabled to continue to work and to fight for their Country.

It would surely be a happy and consoling thought that a Life-boat bearing the historic name of the Regiment should carry on in perpetuity its beneficent activity, under the same inspiration of heroism and self-sacrifice which has brought honour to the Colours of the Regiment.

A MOTOR LIFE-BOAT COSTS £5,250.
Full endowment in perpetuity £12,800.

GEORGE F. SHEE, M.A., Secretary,
ROYAL NATIONAL LIFE-BOAT INSTITUTION,
22, Charing-cross-road, London, W.C.2.

---

in time of trouble, as they have done for the last 80 years, and they must not look in vain. Will you help the Committee to "carry on"?

Patron: H.M. THE KING.
Bankers: Williams Deacon's Bank, Ltd.
Secretary: GERALD F. MAUDE, Esq.,
26, Suffolk Street, Pall Mall East, S.W.1.

Flt. W.O. Marshall
G.H.Q. 20th Division

With reference to your letter of 14th instant. Herewith a record of the doings of this Battalion since it came to FRANCE in November 1914.

A history outline only of the history of the Battalion before it joined the 20th Division is being presented & a complete record of the Battle since it joined the Division in February 1918 is added.

Three photographs are attached viz: one of the Officers of the Battalion in November 1918, one of the Band & one of the TOWERS V.C. as the latter is the sole survivor of R.C.M. Smart of this Battalion I shall be glad if you will kindly return same when you have taken the necessary prints.

If there is any more information which you think is necessary I shall be glad to try and furnish same.

Dalkeith,
Captain & Adjutant,
2nd. Scottish Rifles.

1/1/1919.

Enclosures — 3 photos.

WITH 23RD BRIGADE. 8TH DIVISION.

The 2nd United Rifles Prior to the War were serving in MALTA, and after returning to ENGLAND & Wilting, formed a unit of the 23rd Brigade, 8th Division, sailing for FRANCE on 5th November 1914.

Immediately on arrival at LE HAVRE the Battalion entrained for the front and entered the line near NEUVE EGLISE returning to Divisional Supp. Bns. which had just been in action at the first Battle of YPRES.

In November 1914 the Battalion moved to LAVENTIE SECTOR and did duty in the front line every alternate 3 days throughout the Winter.

After 8 days Preparation at MERVILLE they entered the line near NEUVE CHAPELLE being one of the assaulting Battalions at the Battle of that name on 10th March 1915

With the exception of 12 June N.Y. Somervail all officers became casualties.

Having received their temporary duty from the 1st Battn and drafts from ENGLAND the Battalion took over the Sector at BOIS GRENIER, a Romand in that vicinity till the Battle of FROMELLES 9th May 1915 when they were in support but took no active part in the operations.

Ordinary trench duties were then performed in that Sector till Nov 1915 when the Battalion moved for 2 months rest and HAZEBROUCK and proceeded to the SOMME July 1916.

Next actions were at LA BOISELLE (SOMME) when the Battalion was in gas arr attack on 1st July 1916.

Immediately afterwards they moved to the LOOS SECTOR performing ordinary Trench duties & reliefs till Sept 1916 & returning to SOMME Area, taking in FRITZ TRENCH (SOMME) LE. TRANSLOY. 23rd Oct 1916. afterwards going into rest at AUMATRE.

Returning to the SOMME Area on 1st Jan 1917 the Battalion was in the line in front of MOISLAINS when the Huns retired in March 1917 & following up were at the taking of MOISLAINS. BOUCHAVESNES. TEMPLEUX. LE. GRAND. AIZECOURT-LE-BAS. LIERAMONT. HEUDECOURT. VILLIERS-GUISLAIN. GOUDECOURT etc submiting with a Battalion raid on the outer defences of the HINDENBURG LINE 5th May 1917 immediately afterwards being transferred to MESSINES SECTOR where they took part in the Battle of MESSINES, thereafter moving to YPRES for the third Battle in which they took part on 31st July 1917. Reaching WESHOEK RIDGE their objective & holding ground from attacks till relieved on 1st Aug 1917. The next August the Battalion again held their objective and supported operations taking place from there.

After relief and one months operational duty in the middle of PAASCHENDAELE RIDGE in Dec 1917 remaining there till the middle of January 1918.

In February 1918 the Battalion was transferred from 8th Division to 20th Division on account of Reorganisation.

WITH 59th BRIGADE 20TH DIVISION.

On the 3rd February 1918 while the Battalion was billeted in POPERINGHE orders were received that we would be transferred that day to the 20th Division, 59th Brigade. This only entailed a march of about 15 miles to WIPPENHOEK. Two days later the Battalion moved by Light Railway to MANOR HALT, (ZILLEBEKE) & marched into support positions in the TORR TOP TUNNELS.

Battalion was in the line when until 13th Feby. when the 59th Brigade moved back to LA BELLE HOTESSE Area.

21st March. The Battalion moved into the Corps line at BEAUVOIS.

24th March. Battalion holding the SOMME Canal at VOYENNES. The bridges across the canal had not been properly destroyed. At 08:00 hours the enemy attempted to cross the river, but many of them were knocked out on the river & the remainder fled. At 12:15 hrs. the Battalion on the right fell back allowing the enemy to cross & take our right coy. in the rear. This company under Capt. Stewart, M.C. gallantly counter attacked allowing the remainder of the Battalion to get out of the pocket. Unfortunately only 14 O.Rs. of this coy. under Capt. Stewart got away.

Officer casualties :- 2 killed, 3 wounded & both Medical Officer missing.

25th March. Bn. fought rearguard to positions E. of NESLE. Left flank in the air. Bn. held on in ambush road until enemy were in NESLE immediately behind. Lewis Guns all to Left it span & left flank withdrawn, bombers attack ordered on off at 11:00 hours by Junior was cancelled & the Battalion was out of sight for the night across a certain area of ground. At 14:00 hours the situation was critical as there was no artillery or M.G. support. Enemy approached our position on several occasions signalling to our men to surrender but they were shot down. Battalion tried to get away in small parties. Many were captured trying to get through NESLÉ & many others were killed or wounded by M.G. & shell fire. Only about 50 O.Rs. answered the roll call but a few more were collected at ROYE bringing the strength up to 70 O.Rs.

29th March. Bn. took part in the counter attack on MEZIERES & recaptured prisoners.

Casualties from 21-3-18 to 1-4-18.
Officers: - Killed 4 Wounded 12 W.& Missing 4.
Other Ranks: - Killed, Wounded & Missing 619.

Honours: - Lt. Col. H.C.N. Smith, D.S.O. - Bar to D.S.O.
D.C.Ms. No.12657 Sgt. Duffy E. No.10708 Sgt. O.Wheeler.
M.Ms. No.20128 Cpl.Cullison, No.30303 Sgt. J.Carmichael
No.40716 Pte. L. Johnston.

10th May. Battalion in LENS sector. Enemy answered shelled to attack. Vigorous patrolling was carried out. One officer missing on patrol on 28th May in an encounter with a Boche patrol.

On the 23rd June a raid was carried out by two companies on the enemy's position on the railway embankment.

Raiding party assembled in "no man's land" in shell craters in front of an old french silent forward at 03.05 under an artillery barrage. Some of the enemy were shot down by L.G. & rifle fire & many were killed by the barrage. Mobile charges were thrown into the dugouts completely destroying them & burying many of the enemy. Raiding party returned at 03.45.

Casualties:- 2 O.Rs. missing, 1 killed & 4 wounded. From information obtained from prisoners it was ascertained that all the enemy dugouts at this position (including a company commander's dugout) were destroyed & many Boche killed.

Honours. M.C. Capt. D.F. Campbell (O.C. Raid) M.Ms. No. 42259 Cpl. E. Pow, 41248 A/Cpl. W. Henderson.

1st September. As prisoners had given information that the enemy were evacuating their forward positions a daylight patrol of 2 men under Lieut. A.S. MARTIN went out to the enemy's position on the railway embankment. Arrived there Lt. Martin crept round the embankment by a ruined bridge & saw a Boche N.C.O. sitting in a dugout. He came back & brought his two men forward. He entered the dugout & told the Boche to put his hands up but as the latter seemed to want to fight Lt. Martin shot him through the throat & one of the men also put a bullet through his chest. Identification was obtained & the party walked back across 'no man's land' without being fired on. Lt. Martin was awarded the M.C. for this exploit.

2nd September. Two platoons went forward to occupy the railway embankment. They were successful at first but were heavily bombarded later by shells, & T.Ms. & M.Gs. Had to withdraw: on section missing which had gone off to the right to get in touch with the Green Canaries.

3rd September. Two platoons again established themselves on the embankment but which they were consolidating orders to withdraw were received from Brigade. The missing section of 3 men was found. In endeavouring to cross the canal the clay trenches, two of the men, holding hands endeavouring to cross by a broken bridge, fell into the water. One short had packs & rifles had had to struggle for it. One man drowned & the other managed to swim for it. Another man was wounded & one killed.

30th September. Battalion in the Avion sector. Information was received that the Huns were withdrawing from their front trench system. Numerous fires were observed along the whole front. Our patrols were very active upon this.

2nd October. On patrol under 2/Lt G. Smith MC reported that the Huns had evacuated the railway embankment at MERICOURT, and in consequence of the one Company well forward and occupied the same. The Support Company then moved up & passing through the new front line advanced across the BULLRING and joined line Save 500 + in front of the Railway Embankment.

3rd October. During the heavy machine gun fire from MERICOURT, which the Boche still held, the Battalion on our right was unable to advance & keep in touch with us. As result of this our right flank was in the air, and in order to clear up the situation one of the reserve companies was pushed forward to the outskirts of MERICOURT so as to form a defensive flank, until the flank Battalion could come up. In the course of this operation 2 prisoners of the 164th Regt were taken. The Boche now evidently very outnumbered by this advance as no new front garrisons of front resisting in the dugouts along the Rly tunnel they had advanced.

4th & 5th October. Although the situation at MERICOURT had been considerably improved the Boche still held a number of posts in the Village. During this two days our patrols were active. Our right flank Battalion were unable to gain touch with the flank Battalion, who had apparently been unable to leave their original front line.

6th October. During the morning this clearing patrols were pushed out

30245 Pte. James Towers 2/@ SCOTTISH RIFLES.

VICTORIA CROSS.

At MERICOURT on the 6th October a platoon which had worked forward into the village got cut off by Machine Guns located on three sides. Owing to other platoons working through the village having been driven in, it was essential that the platoon should be informed of the situation and withdrawn.

The first runner sent with the message was wounded as soon as he exposed himself. The second man who made the attempt was killed. Three other attempts to reach the isolated platoon failed — owing to heavy Machine Gun fire as soon as any man was seen.

Then Private TOWERS volunteered to try and get the message to them. As soon as he showed himself heavy Machine Gun fire was opened on him, but in spite of this he went straight on, running from cover to cover, and eventually delivered the message. He remained with the platoon until dusk when he led the platoon back to the Company. He showed the greatest courage and determination and an utter disregard for his personal safety. He set a magnificent example to his comrades.

6th October (cont) to various ant the machine nests in MERICOURT which were hindering our advance. The patrol obtained its objective whereabouts it held on until ordered to withdraw, but the other through no fault of their own was unable to support them.

Pte Forrest attempted to get orders out to the former patrol which was under the command of Sgt W.B. Jack, was frustrated by the heavy machine gun fire of the two Runners who attempted to convey back the wounded patrol one was killed and one was wounded and the wounded patrol one was killed, and one was wounded and the remaining two were unable to reach them owing to the intense fire which was opened as soon as any one was exposed. Hereupon *Pte No. 3025 Pte James Forrest V.C. a Runner volunteered to take the message to the patrol. As soon as he showed himself hostile machine guns opened from everywhere, but in spite of this he went straight on, running from cover to cover, and eventually delivered his message to Sgt W.B. Jack. He remained with the Patrol until dusk when he led them back to the company. He showed the greatest courage and determination, well knowing that in volunteering for the task he would have to run the gauntlet of the two machine guns. He failed in the last 20yds of the journey. In this action Forrest received his mortal injuries.

On the night of the 6th the Battalion was relieved by the 6th Bn/90 of the 12th Division, and after relief proceeded to billets in BERLE in two hours.

*Award attached

Honours:- VICTORIA CROSS :- No. 3025 Pte. J. Forrest —
           MILITARY   2Lt. W. B. Jack
           BAR to the M.M.   A6.43339 Pte. W. McGinley
                             No. 10257 Pte. J. Allan
           M.M.   No. 514790 Cpl S. Smith
           M.M.

Casualties. From 30.9.18. to 6.10.18.
             Officers   2   wounded
             Other Ranks 7   Killed
                         10   wounded.

October 31st. Bn. in CAMBRAI waiting to take part in the general advance.

1st to 11th November. Bn. marching nearly every day, all ranks doing to get in touch with the enemy. Armistice declared while Bn. was at JENLAIN.

After nov. 11th the Bn. marched forward by stages finally resting at TAISNIERES.

2nd BATTALION

THE SCOTTISH RIFLES

FEBRUARY 1 9 1 8

Ap '19

59th Brigade
20th Division.

WAR DIARY
or
INTELLIGENCE SUMMARY.

(Erase heading not required.)

Army Form C. 2118.

Place	Date	Hour	Summary of Events and Information	Remarks and references to Appendices
	1st Feby. to 2nd Feby.		Battalion supplied large working parties for work in forward area near WIELTJE.	
	3rd Feby.		The Battalion was transferred from 8th Division to 59th Brigade, 20th Division & moved into huts about 2 miles from POPERINGHE.	O.O.40
	4th Feby.		Cleaning up.	
	5th Feby.		Battalion moved into support positions in the CAMERON COVERT Sector. Accommodated in tunnels.	O.O.41
	5th to 6th Feby.		Large working parties supplied from support positions for work under R.E.s	
	9th Feby.	6 p.m.	The battalion relieved the 1/Auckland Bn. in the line between the REUTELBEEK & STEENBEEK streams. Relief complete about 9 p.m.	O.O.42
	11th Feby.		Battalion remained in the line until night of 11/12th Feby. when it was relieved by the 11th K.R.R.C. & moved back to support positions.	O.O.43
			Working parties were supplied from support positions until Bn. was relieved on night of 13th/14th inst. by 6th K.S.L.I. 60th Bde.	O.O.44

WAR DIARY
or
INTELLIGENCE SUMMARY.
(Erase heading not required.)

Army Form C. 2118.

Place	Date	Hour	Summary of Events and Information	Remarks and references to Appendices
			On relief by 6th K.S.L.I. the battalion marched to FORESTER CAMP. Rained heavily all day & night of 13th & men were drenched. Good camp & fires awaited them.	O.O.44
	14th Feby.		Battalion entrained for BLARINGHEM area. Arrived in billets about 8 p.m. Billets fairly good but very scattered.	O.O.45
	15th Feby.		Training was started.	
	17th Feby.		G.O.C. 59th Infy. Bde. (Brigadier General H.H.G. Hyslop D.S.O.) inspected the battalion & regtl. transport & welcomed them to the Brigade.	
			Battalion training	
			The battalion 20th Division was transferred to the 5th Army & moved by rail from STEENBECQUE to NESLE (Ref. Map. AMIENS 17 - 3K 95.15) on 20th February - a train journey of approximately 13 hours. Detrained at NESLE & marched to BEAULIEU 5K 99.90. BEAULIEU was vacated by the Germans during the SOMME retirement & a few houses have been blown up	

WAR DIARY or INTELLIGENCE SUMMARY.

Army Form C. 2118.

(Erase heading not required.)

Place	Date	Hour	Summary of Events and Information	Remarks and references to Appendices
	February		Battalion all in billets at 5.30 a.m. 21st February.	
			Billets were fairly comfortable, every man having a bed - made by the Germans.	
			Training until 2nd March.	

2nd BATTALION

THE SCOTTISH RIFLES

MARCH 1918

59th Brigade.
20th Division.

WAR DIARY
or
INTELLIGENCE SUMMARY.
(Erase heading not required.)

Army Form C. 2118.

Place	Date	Hour	Summary of Events and Information	Remarks and references to Appendices
	1918			
	~~March~~ Feby.		Battalion ~~arrived~~ all in billets at 5.30 a.m. 21st February. Billets were fairly comfortable, every man having a bed - made by the Germans.	
CHAULNES			Training until 2nd March.	
	2 March		Moved by route march to CHAULNES, Sheet 66d. A.4.a. Village behind old Boche lines & in ruins. Continued here doing working parties on roads. 3 Coys per day the other doing training.	
	20th		Moved back to BEAULIEU our place in CHAULNES being taken by 11th K.R.R.C.	
	21st		At 5 A.M. a tremendous bombardment was heard in the direction of ST. QUENTIN. At dawn the order was received to be ready to move at a moment's notice. At 12.30 p.m. the Battn. paraded for distribution of Medal ribbons to each by Genl. Douglas-Smith Comdg. 20th Divn. At 2.0 p.m. Battn. marched via LANGUEVOISIN to UGNY about 16 miles. Arrived there at 9 p.m. Billeted in huts.	

WAR DIARY or INTELLIGENCE SUMMARY

Army Form C. 2118.

Place	Date	Hour	Summary of Events and Information	Remarks and references to Appendices
BEAUVOIS	March 22nd	1 A.M.	Order "XVIII Corps man battle stations" received. Bttn. marched to Corps Line (4 miles). This line was strongly wired but trenches only not dug. Work on trenches was at once begun. 59th Bde. held the line from VAUX to VILLEVECQUE, 60th & 61st Bdes. being on the Right. Some shelling during morning.	
		1. P.M.	The Bde. was ordered to concentrate near FORESTE for a counter attack (marched 5 miles). No counter attack was made and just before dark the Bde. marched to DOUILLY to man the D.Y. ~~Line~~ Switch (5 miles). At this time the Germans were said to be in BEAUVOIS, having turned the left flank of the 61st Divn.	
VOYENNES	23rd	2 A.M.	The Brigade started to retire to the line of the SOMME Canal getting there at 6 A.M. (7 miles). 9 Sco. Rif. held the bridge at VOYENNES with canal bank for 1000x to N. of it. 11th K.R.R.C. on R. 11th R.B. on Left. Trenches deepened & improved. Some Germans appeared on the ridge about midday & there was shelling in the afternoon but no attack followed.	

WAR DIARY
or
INTELLIGENCE SUMMARY.

(Erase heading not required.)

Army Form C. 2118.

Place	Date	Hour	Summary of Events and Information	Remarks and references to Appendices
VOYENNES	1918 March 24 (Sun.)		B Coy. under Capt. Stewart held the bridge, with A Coy holding the canal to the North. C Coy was in support and D Coy. in 2 redoubts on the high ground to West. At 8 A.M. about 50 Germans tried to rush the remains of the bridge under cover of their smoke (?); they were nearly all knocked out. Later the enemy heavily shelled our trenches about the bridge. At about 12.15 P.M. the K.R.R.C. on our right fell back allowing the Germans to cross the canal on their front. The enemy got into VOYENNES and opened M.G. fire on B. Coy from the rear. The situation was now impossible and Capt. Stewart skillfully withdrew the remnants of his company (24 men only) after a most gallant defence. The enemy had meantime crossed the canal at BETHENCOURT about 2 miles on our left, and the brigade fell back fighting a rear guard action to a line in front of NESLE. This line was hardly dug at all as there was no time. Amongst many other casualties 2/Lt GRAHAM M.C. killed, 2/Lt MACKAY, — MARSHALL, — GOURLAY } were missing, Revd HUNTER C.F. wounded, Capt JONES R.A.M.C. & Corpl FORD missing	

WAR DIARY
or
INTELLIGENCE SUMMARY.
(Erase heading not required.)

Army Form C. 2118.

Instructions regarding War Diaries and Intelligence Summaries are contained in F. S. Regs., Part II. and the Staff Manual respectively. Title pages will be prepared in manuscript.

Place 1918	Date	Hour	Summary of Events and Information	Remarks and references to Appendices
NESLE	March 25		The line held by the Battn. was from QUIQUERY on the R. to the Railway on the left. It consisted of a trench (unwired) with a sunken road about 150x in rear of it. 184 Bde held line on our R. and a unit known as Divl. Reinforcement Battn. were supposed to be on our left. A marshy stream thickly wooded ran from our R. back towards NESLE. At daybreak patrols confirmed that there was nobody on our left, report was made to brigade and a reply was received to the effect that the left was all right. As Germans could be seen moving round our flank in large numbers, "A" Coy under W.H. Grant was turned back to form a defensive flank. At about 11 am a French M.G. Coy (10 guns) reported to us and came into action at QUIQUERY. Their battery fired over our heads onto the NESLE Road & gave invaluable assistance. By noon the situation was critical. A Coy after a gallant fight were driven back into the Sunken road and the enemy now right on our flank kept up an intense M.G. fire on every part of our position. No assistance was given by our artillery although the NESLE road was swarming with Germans.	

Place	Date	Hour	Summary of Events and Information	Remarks and references to Appendices
	March			
NESLE	25(c'd)	2 p.m.	Situation now desperate, enemy firing straight down sunken road. The men began to get away by small parties up the stream towards NESLE. This was the only way of escape now open. By 2.15 the last man was out of the sunken road, but many were caught by M.G. & shell fire as they went up the valley. Most of the survivors appear to have gone into NESLE and were probably captured by the Germans who had by this time got right round. Only 7 officers and 55 men got back to the Brigade. The gallant fight made by the battalion undoubtedly barred the road to NESLE to the enemy for several hours after the troops on our left had fallen back. It may even have saved the Brigade on our Right whose flank would have been completely turned had the Germans succeeded in working up the stream towards NESLE.	

WAR DIARY or INTELLIGENCE SUMMARY.

Army Form C. 2118

(Erase heading not required.)

Place	Date	Hour	Summary of Events and Information	Remarks and references to Appendices
QUENELLES	March 26		During night 25/26 the Brigade collected on outskirts of ROYE. Marched to QUENELLES at dawn & went into billets. Turned out at noon to man a ridge behind village. Brought in again at dusk.	
		9 p.m.	Marched out to FOLIE remained in village in support to 50th Divn. K.R.R.C. out in front. R.B. in village	
FOLIE	27th		Moved back to some old gun pits behind village. Lay there all day. Owing to some misunderstanding 50th Divn. evacuated their trenches & Germans came on slightly. Line re-established	
	28th	6 p.m.	Relieved by French troops. Marched to wood near MEZIERES. Stayed there for the night. Weather cold & wet. Men & officers much exhausted	
	29th		Brigade moved in early morning to hold MEZIERES in conjunction with the French. K.R.R.C. in the trenches. 9 Scottish Rifles in support. The battn. at this time consisted of about 70 men. Coy near AMIENS road. 1 Coy and H.Q. in VILLERS. Enemy attacked about noon, were driven out by a counter attack at 4 p.m. After a good deal of shelling, Germans again advanced and our troops fell back gradually to a line on the high ground E. of DOMART. The 3 brigades dug in in line on a front of about 3000x. 60' Bde on right, 59th centre, 61st on left.	

A5834. Wt. W4973/M687. 750,000. 8/16. D. D. & L. Ltd. Forms/C.2118/13.

WAR DIARY
or
INTELLIGENCE SUMMARY.

(Erase heading not required.)

Army Form C. 2118.

Place	Date	Hour	Summary of Events and Information	Remarks and references to Appendices
	1918 March 30	8 AM	The French line seem to be falling back from a large wood on our R. flank, and German cavalry patrols entered it. Our line fell back, but troops of 2nd Cavalry Division drove the enemy out of the wood and our line was restored by the evening. Wet weather. H.Q. in Quarry on road E. of DOMART.	
	31 (Sun)		The night was quiet as usual but at midday the German shelling on Rifleman Wood & trenches in front of it became heavy. Troops on R & L. fell back and by 2 p.m. our line was on the slopes below Rifleman Wood. The enemy pushed forward M. Guns on both flanks and in the evening our line fell back over the LUCE stream to position on both sides of DOMART. H.Q. in a cellar in the village. The strength of the battn. was now 4 Officers including (C.O. & Adjt) 55 O.R. The casualties since March 21st were 19 officers — 10 wounded 9 missing 619 other ranks — 15 killed 92 wounded 512 missing	

G.P. Wright Capt. & Adjutant,
1 Scottish Rifles.

Headquarters
30th Division

Herewith War Diary for
month of April 1918.

7th May 1918

To:-

Lieut-colonel
Commanding 2scottish Rifles

WAR DIARY or INTELLIGENCE SUMMARY

2 Scottish Rifles

Place	Date 1918	Hour	Summary of Events and Information	Remarks and references to Appendices
DOMART	April 1st	9 A.M.	2/ Scottish Rifles held bank of stream on R. of village, 11th K.R.R.C. in centre & 11th R.B. on left. A mixed force mostly Canadian Cavalry under Brig. Genl. Seeley attacked the Germans in Rifleman wood and drove them on to the top of the high ground. At about 11 A.M. a long column of Cavalry in fours rode down the main street of DOMART in full view of the Boche. This caused the village to be heavily shelled. The cavalry got out at a gallop. Afternoon fairly quiet. The long looked for orders for relief arrived at last and the brigade withdrew at dusk. The battn. numbered 4 officers & 60 men.	

WAR DIARY or INTELLIGENCE SUMMARY.

Army Form C. 2118.

Place	Date	Hour	Summary of Events and Information	Remarks and references to Appendices
QUEVAUVILLERS	1918 April 2nd		Lorries conveyed the Bde to a back area S.W. of Amiens. Got in at 5 A.M. Troops put down in a field but afterwards moved to billets.	
"	3rd	1.30 p.m.	Battn. marched to AUMONT (7 miles) and went into billets.	
AUMONT	4th		Rested and cleaned up.	
"	5th		Brig. Genl. Ovens, who had just taken over Bde. inspected Battn. in billets. Draft of 6 officers & 392 o.r. arrived. Of these 218 came from 4th Battn. K.O.S.B. remainder from R.S. Fusiliers, none of our own men. The K.O.S.B. men of poor physique & disgracefully turned out.	
"	6th		Inspection of draft by C.O.	
"	7th (Sun)		Church parades	
"	8th		Company parades	
"	9th		Route march about 5 miles	

WAR DIARY
or
INTELLIGENCE SUMMARY.

(Erase heading not required.)

Army Form C. 2118.

Place	Date 1918	Hour	Summary of Events and Information	Remarks and references to Appendices
RAMBURES	April 10	8 A.M.	The Divn. moved northwards. Battn. marched to RAMBURES about 15 miles got in about 3.30 p.m. Battn. H.Q. in the Chateau. About 100 men rejoined from leave & classes.	
~~DARGN~~ DARGNIES	11	8.15 AM	Marched to DARGNIES about 11 miles got in at 2.30 P.M. 8 officers joined from 9th Scottish Rifles.	
"	12		Company parades.	
"	13		" "	
"	14		Church "	
"	15.		Draft of 223 O.R. (mainly K.O.S.B.) proceeds to Pont Remy (Corps Reinforcement Camp) Bn marches to and billets night 15/16 to field fire next day.	
"	16		Field firing at Bn marched back to DARGNIES arriving about 4 p.m. Major Sandilands arrives from 15th Division	
"	17.		Coy. Parades. " V.B. Gray M.C. joins Battn from S.O. School	
"	18.		Bn embusses near WOINCOURT at 10 a.m and debusses at TINCQUES at 5.30 p.m. & billets at BERLES-MONCHY	
BERLES MONCHY.	19		Coy. Parades. Capt. Actg Major T.B.G. Foster joins Battn.	

WAR DIARY
or
INTELLIGENCE SUMMARY.
(Erase heading not required.)

Army Form C. 2118.

Place	Date	Hour	Summary of Events and Information	Remarks and references to Appendices
BERLES MONCHY	20	-	Coy. Parades. - Visit from Divisional Commander expected but cancelled. Conference on Training at Corps H.Q.	
"	21	-	(Sunday) Training 9am - 12 am	
"	22	-	Coy. Parades.	
"	23	-	" " Lt. Col. Hyde-Smith receives orders to proceed to U.K. (Major A. Macfarlane joins Bn. Lt. NRM Munro " " 2 Lt. Henning " "	
"	24	-	Coy. Parades. Lecture on Anti-aircraft Lewis gun sights etc by expert from Corps H.Q. Lecture by Education Officer. (Lt. Col. H. Smith leaves for U.K.)	
"	25		Coy Parades & Musketry	
"	26		" " & "	
"	27		" " & "	
"	28		(Sunday) Kit Inspections - Church Parades. Bn marches to Tincques to see Demonstration by Special Corps Platoon.	

WAR DIARY or INTELLIGENCE SUMMARY.

(Erase heading not required.)

Army Form C. 2118.

Place	Date	Hour	Summary of Events and Information	Remarks and references to Appendices
BERLES between ARRAS & ST. POL on main ARRAS road (LENS sheet)	April 29th		Training on Coy parade grounds	
	30th		Battalion Field Day on 61st Bde Training Area N of TINQUES. Practised Field Firing by coys.	

T B S Forster Major
for. Lieut. Colonel
Commanding 2/Scottish Rifles

Headquarters
20th Division
—

Herewith War Diary for month
of May.

2/6/18.

D. Mitchell
Captain
for Commanding 20thotst Rifles

WAR DIARY or INTELLIGENCE SUMMARY.

2 Scottish Rifles

Vol 42

Place	Date	Hour	Summary of Events and Information	Remarks and references to Appendices
BERLES	MAY 1st		Usual training. Received orders to move to SOUCHEZ - CARENCY area on 2nd May.	
	2nd		Battalion marched to ALBERTA CAMP (about 10 miles) arriving about 6 p.m. All in nissen huts just W of VIMY RIDGE. Huts are good & men are fairly comfortable.	
	3rd to 10th		Battalion in Corps Reserve training in ALBERTA CAMP. All routes to N & S were reconnoitred in case of enemy attacking on the flanks & trying to turn the VIMY RIDGE flanks. G.O.C. 3rd Division. Major General G.G.S. Carey, C.B., presented medal ribbons to N C Os & men for gallant conduct during the withdrawal from 21st march to 30th march. Sgt. O. Wheeler D.C.M. Sgt. C. Duffy D.C.M. Cpl. A. Wilson M.M. Cpl. J. Carmichael M.M. Pte. L. Johnston M.M. Battalion moved into the LENS sector on night of 10/11th May. Battalion on right of Brigade.	
	11th to 13th		In right sub-section LENS section. On night of 12/13th a party of 20 of the enemy approached our outpost line but a wiring party under Lieut. A.S. Martin forced them back to their lines. Enemy put over a considerable number of gas shells. Battalion moved into Brigade support in LIEVIN on night of 13/14th May.	
	14th to 16th		In Brigade support. Battalion all on working parties. Major R. Macfarlane, D Coy wounded on 15th by a shell.	

WAR DIARY
or
INTELLIGENCE SUMMARY.
(Erase heading not required.)

Army Form C. 2118.

Instructions regarding War Diaries and Intelligence Summaries are contained in F. S. Regs., Part II. and the Staff Manual respectively. Title pages will be prepared in manuscript.

Place	Date	Hour	Summary of Events and Information	Remarks and references to Appendices
LENS SECTOR			Battalion moved into left sub section on the night of 16/17th	
	17th to 19th		In left sub section. 11th R.B. carried out a small raid from our line but were unsuccessful in securing any prisoners.	
			2Lieut. R.P. Conochie was killed on the 18th	
			Battalion relieved by 4th Somerset L.I. on night of 19/20th & moved back to ALBERTA CAMP. All in camp about 4 a.m.	
	20th		Moved into left sub-section of AVION sector on night of 20/21st relieving 6th K.S.L.I.s. 60th Brigade.	
	21st to 24th		In AVION sector. Enemy sent over a considerable number of gas shells. Lieut. A.S. Martin, 2Lieuts. Wishart, Grant & McIntosh all gassed.	
			Gas was sent out from our lines on night of 23/24th. Enemy made no retaliation.	
			Moved into Bde. support on night of 24/25th. Battalion in RED TRENCH & remained there until 27th. Battalion all on working parties.	
	28th to 29th		Battalion moved into right sub sector on night of 27/28th. Patrol under 2Lieut Fleming C. Coy. ran into an enemy M.G. post & were fired on. Only one of the patrol got back to our lines	
			Battalion relieved by 12th Rifle Brigade on night of 29th/30th & marched back into Corps Reserve in COLUMBIA CAMP.	

Place	Date	Hour	Summary of Events and Information	Remarks and references to Appendices
	30th & 31st		Shortly after Battalion arrived enemy put a few shells round the camp. On 30th Battalion employed cleaning up generally. Training commenced on 31st.	

Sandilands
Lieut. Colonel,
Commanding 2nd Scottish Rifles

Reference sheet LENS 1/100,000   2nd Btn Artists Rifles OTC no 3

1. The 59th Inf Bde will move into Divisional Reserve in the SOUCHEZ-CARENCY area tomorrow 2nd May, 1918.

2. The Btn will form up in column of route on the ST-POL-ARRAS Road at 2.40 pm in the following order and march to billets camp: HQ. "B". "C". "D". "A".

3. Route: Road junction HAUTE-AYESNES-VILLERS-AU-BOIS.

4. Head of column at head of road south of Q in Italian (SAY) facing 6.

5. An interval of 200 yards will be maintained between companies. Interval will march 200 yards in rear of "A" Coy.

6. Dress: field service marching order off steel helmets will be filled up and worn off steel helmets will be worn.

7. Rendering being kept out under LA 135, except officers will turn up 200 yards in rear of Transport they will be accommodated at the transport lines in animals in new area.

8. Blankets will be rolled in bundles and stacked outside Coys HQ by 12 noon to be collected by motor lorry.

9. Officers Mess kits will be ready to be collected from Companies by NCO Mess by motor lorry at 1 pm.

10. Officers valises will be stacked outside officers' mess by 11 am. to be collected by Regimental transport.

11. All other kits will still be carried on Gas appliances & AA positions will be known by days will apart all in camp on arrival in new area.

12.
13. Acknowledge

O Dubuis Captain
Adjutant 2/Artists Rifles
2/5/18

War Diary Vimy 17th May 1918
Reference Map: Trench Map Sheets 36b NW & SW 1/10,000, 36 (LENS)

1. The Bn. will relieve the 11th R. Bde. in the Right Subsector tonight 17th May.
2. Bn. will take over the line as under:-

	1st Line	2nd Line	MLR
Right Subsect	"C"	"B"	
Centre Subsect	"A"	"D"	
Left Subsect	"B"	"C"	

3. Coys "A" & "D" will move off at the following times:-

"D" day 9.15 p.m.
"A" "   9.30 "
"B" "   9.40 "
B.H.Q.   10.0 p.m.

4. Guides will meet the Bn. will be
advanced to Batln.
"D" Coy. H.Q. at men Souris & AVION trench
junction on Jetties in the
Catacombs Map Ref. T.3.c.5.7.
"B" "   1.Batln AVION trench
"A" "   1.Batln TAYLOR "
         2.Batln ADEPT "
"B" "   1.Batln TAYLOR "
         2.Batln ACTRESS "
"A" "   1.Batln ADEPT "
         2.Batln T.2.c.10
"B" "   1.Batln AVION trench
         2.Batln ADEPT "
Coy H.Q. T.2.c.7.1.
3.Battn AVION trench 5.6. actress
Battn Headquarters T.1.d.2.1.
1.Batln relieving — relieving & across Avenue
Hert By G Batln   S. ACTRESS trench
                                is along 3/8 BdR

WAR DIARY
or
INTELLIGENCE SUMMARY.
(Erase heading not required.)

Army Form C. 2118.

2 Scottish Rifles

Vol 43

Place	Date	Hour	Summary of Events and Information	Remarks and references to Appendices
	June 1st to 4th		Battalion in COLUMBIA CAMP training. Enemy shelled the camp practically every night & although a few shells landed near the huts there were no casualties.	
			On the night of 4/8th June the Bn. relieved the 7th Somerset L.I. in the support positions in the LENS section. Enemy sent over a number of BLUE CROSS Gas shells which caused B.H.Q. personnel to put on box respirators. Relief complete at 1 a.m. 8th.	O.O.15
	8th June		Quiet day. Brigadier General Baylay visited the Bn.	
	9th 10th June		Very little enemy shelling. Bn. in Support.	
			On the night of 10/11th June Bn. relieved the 11th K.R.R.C. in the right sub. section. Enemy put some gas shells into LIEVIN. Relief complete at 1.30 a.m.	O.O.15A
	11th to 13th		Fairly quiet. Patrols were out on the front every night but no enemy were encountered.	
	14th		Quiet day. At about 12 M.N. 14/15th were ordered to alter our dispositions slightly so that there was more defence in depth. A Coy were brought back about 400 yards. About 4 a.m. the enemy put up many coloured lights & opened a bombardment on	

WAR DIARY or INTELLIGENCE SUMMARY

Army Form C. 2118.

Place	Date	Hour	Summary of Events and Information	Remarks and references to Appendices
June			our front positions. No action followed. Bombardment lasted about ½ hour. Had only six ~~men~~ casualties (wounded)	
15th & 16th			Quiet. Very little shelling. On the night of 16/17th June the Bn. was relieved by the 6th D.C.L.I. Relief complete at 3 a.m. & Bn. moved by light railway to SOUCHEZ HUTS.	O.O. 16
17th			Bn. resting during the day. At night marched to support positions in the AVION sector in relief of 6th K.S.L.I.	OO. 17
19th			Dispositions had to be altered on night of 18th. The three Bns. have to be in the line at the same time disposed in depth to the RED LINE. "D" Coy. moved into front line on the right of the Brigade front & "C" Coy moved into support to "D" Coy. Rained heavily during the move & the men got fairly wet.	
19th			"A" & "B" Coys. moved along the RED LINE to the SOUTH & B.H.Q. also moved thus completing the new dispositions. The Bn. now holds the right sub section of the AVION sector, 11th K.R.R.C. in the centre & the 11th R.B. on the left.	

WAR DIARY
or
INTELLIGENCE SUMMARY.
(Erase heading not required.)

Army Form C. 2118.

Instructions regarding War Diaries and Intelligence Summaries are contained in F. S. Regs., Part II. and the Staff Manual respectively. Title pages will be prepared in manuscript.

Place	Date	Hour	Summary of Events and Information	Remarks and references to Appendices
	20th to 22nd June.		Very active patrolling with a view to carrying out a raid on the enemy's positions. Raid carried out on morning of 23rd at 3.5 a.m. by A & B Coys. All arrangements were carried out without a hitch. Although it was bright moonlight both Coys. got into assembly positions without being observed. The artillery barrage opened on the railway embankment punctual to time & the Coys. moved forward immediately it lifted. A few of the enemy were seen running away on the W. side of the embankment. Lewis Guns were opened on them & many of them ran into our box barrage. Two were killed before they could get away, one by 2/Lt. A. Duncan, "A" Coy. & identification was obtained. Many of the enemy tried to get out of their deep dugouts but mobile charges carried by the R.E. were thrown down the dugouts which blew them up. The raiding party returned to our lines about 3.40 a.m. No prisoners were brought back but the main object of the raid i.e. to obtain identification, kill as many	O.O.14

Place	Date	Hour	Summary of Events and Information	Remarks and references to Appendices
	24th		of the enemy as possible & blow in his dugouts, was carried out. Our casualties were 1 O.R. killed, 7 O.Rs. wounded & 2 O.Rs. missing (Sgt. Henderson D.C.M. "A" Coy. & Pte. Gregory "B" Coy.) Quiet during the day. Our artillery carried out a gas shell bombardment of the enemy's lines, about 10.30 p.m.	
	25th & 26th		Artillery fairly active on both sides. G.O.C. Division came round the line in the afternoon of 26th. Bn. was relieved by the 12th R.Bs on night of 26th/27th June & moved by light railway to SOUCHEZ HUTS. All in camp about 4.30 a.m. 27th June. A mild kind of fever has caused many of our men to be sent to hospital, about 150 altogether.	O.O. 20
	27th to 30th		Bn. doing working parties practically every day. Many men & officers have got this new fever including C.O. Brigadier General Bayley inspected the Bn. on the morning of 30th June.	

D. Wright. Capt. & Adjt.
for O.C. 2nd Scottish Rifles

WAR DIARY or INTELLIGENCE SUMMARY.

(Erase heading not required.)

Army Form C. 2118.

2 Scottish Rifles

Vol 44

Place	Date	Hour	Summary of Events and Information	Remarks and references to Appendices
	July 1918			
	1st to 5th		Bn. in SOUCHEZ HUTS doing working parties & cleaning up & improving camp. A Bde Race Meeting was held on 2nd July. Bn. won three 2nd prizes & one 1st for transport shows.	
	5th		Bn. should have relieved the 12th Kings Liverpool Regt. on night of 5/6th but relief was postponed owing to a proposed Gas Beam attack. At 8.30 p.m. a telephone message was received that relief would take place. Tram arrangements were cancelled & the Bn. marched into the line. Guides were lost & relief was not complete until 3 a.m. 6th.	O.O. 26.
	6th to 14th		Very quiet tour. Bosche aeroplanes dropped about 6 bombs near B.H.Q, possibly trying to hit batteries. Relieved by 12th Kings Liverpool Regt. on night of 14/15th. Relief complete at 3 a.m. Bn. moved to LORETTE CAMP by light railway. (Casualties for tour	O.O. 27
	15th		In camp during the day & relieved the 12th R.B.s at night. Thunderstorm during relief & trenches & dugouts were flooded	O.O. 28
	17th		A fighting patrol of 1 platoon & 2 sections under Lt. Brassington, Lieut. E.F. Smith, & 2/Lieut. G. Smith went out on night of 17/18th to try & capture some of the enemy posts.	

WAR DIARY or INTELLIGENCE SUMMARY.

Army Form C. 2118.

Place	Date	Hour	Summary of Events and Information	Remarks and references to Appendices
	18th		but the night was too dark & the ground too muddy for good patrolling. A Gas T.M. bombardment was carried out on the enemy's positions on night of 18/19th. Patrols were not able to go out.	
	19th		Same patrol as went out on night of 17/18th went out again on night of 19/20th. Patrol made its way up enemy communication trench to the Railway embankment. One or two unoccupied enemy posts were entered & a notice board & an enemy grenade were obtained. Our side of the embankment was found to have been thickly wired. This had apparently been done since our raid on the morning of 23rd June. Patrol returned to our line about 3 a.m. without having obtained identification. An enemy deserter gave himself up to the 11th R.B's on the left of the Brigade front on night of 18th. Rumble of a bombardment heard in the South.	
	21st		One of our patrols came near an enemy post & bombs were exchanged. None of the patrol were wounded.	
	22nd		Col. Sadilands back from leave. At night one platoon of each	

WAR DIARY or INTELLIGENCE SUMMARY.

Army Form C. 2118.

Place	Date	Hour	Summary of Events and Information	Remarks and references to Appendices
	24th		Battalion of the 60th Brigade carried out a combined raid. One prisoner & an enemy M.G. obtained. 11th K.R.R.C. also carried out a raid under cover of a smoke cloud. An enemy M.G. was captured but no identification was obtained. Bn. relieved by 12th R.B's on night of 24/25th & moved to LORETTE CAMP. C & D Coys. by train, A & B Coys. by march route. Casualties from 16th to 24th. 1 O.R. (Sgt. McNeil) killed on relief night 24th whilst going down communication trench.	O.O. 29
	25th to 31st		In LORETTE CAMP training. Training very much hampered for the first three days owing to heavy rain. Lieut. General Sir Aylmer Hunter Weston K.C.B. D.S.O. (the Corps Commander) visited the Battalion on 29th to see training. Recreational training carried out in the afternoon & boxing tournaments in the evening. Semi-finals for Brigade boxing competition fought on 31st & the Bn. is fairly well represented. Brigade Ceremonial parade on 31st.	

V. Sandilands
Lieut. Colonel
Commanding 2nd Scottish Rifles

WAR DIARY or INTELLIGENCE SUMMARY.

(Erase heading not required.)

2nd Sco Rifles

Army Form C. 2118.

Vol 45

Place	Date	Hour	Summary of Events and Information	Remarks and references to Appendices
LORETTE CAMP.	August 1st to 2nd		Training, recreational & otherwise. Battalion moved into the right sub section of the LENS Section on the night of the 2/3rd in relief of the 12th Kings Liverpool Regt. Two coys. moved by light railway & two coys by march route. Train had a collision but there were no casualties.	O.O.30
	3rd to 6th		Fairly quiet tour. The Corps Commander came round the line on the 6th. A Coy. relieved B Coy. in the front line on the night of 6/7th.	
	7th to 11th		Every day fairly quiet. Usual patrol activity. Men bathe in a pond behind the support line. Bn. was relieved on the night of 11/12th by the 4th D.C.L.I. & moved into camp for a day.	O.O.31
	12th to 19th		Relieved the 12th R.Bs. in AVION Section on the night of 12/13th. Numerous changes in dispositions took place. The Brigade front was held by two battalions in the line & one in reserve in LORETTE CAMP. The Battalion moved into reserve, one coy. on the 18th & three coys. on the 19th. B Coy. went out on patrol on the night of 18/19th to find out if the enemy had withdrawn. Enemy was found to be holding the embankment & bombs were thrown & machine guns opened on the patrol. All got back without casualties.	O.O.32 O.O.33.
	20th to 28th		Training &c. in LORETTE CAMP. Battalion sports held on the 24th. Prizes given of War Bonds. Bn. relieved the 11th R.Bs. in the AVION section on the night of 28/29th. B Coy. front line, A Coy. support, C & D Coys in reserve.	O.O.34
	29th to 31st		Many rumours of the enemy having withdrawn but patrols still report that he is still there. Usual patrolling.	

U. Sandilands Lt. Col.
Commanding 2nd Scottish Rifles.

WAR DIARY or INTELLIGENCE SUMMARY.

2 Scottish Rifles
Vol 46

Army Form C. 2118.

Place	Date September 1918	Hour	Summary of Events and Information	Remarks and references to Appendices
TRENCHES AVION Section Left Bn.	1st		Prisoners taken in the LENS Section on our left stated that the enemy infantry had gone back leaving only 35 men per regiment to cover the work of the pioneers who had to blow up the cellars in LENS. Lieut. MARTIN & two men of "A" Coy. went forward in daylight to find out if the enemy were still holding the railway embankment. He found one of the enemy sitting in a dugout & ordered him to put his hands up. As the Boche appeared to be about to offer resistance Lt. Martin shot him in the throat. No more enemy were seen. A identification which proved to be normal was brought back.	
	2nd	3 p.m.	Two platoons of "B" Coy. went forward to try & occupy the railway embankment. Two platoons of the 11th K.R.R.C. on our right went forward at the same time. The enemy offered some resistance throwing rifle grenades & opening with Machine Guns mostly on the 11th K.R.R.C. & both parties had to withdraw. One section was sent off along the railway embankment to the left to get in touch with the battalion there. This section failed to return on the 2nd. One sergeant killed. Platoons got back to our lines.	
	3rd	6 p.m.	Two platoons of "A" Coy. went forward to again try & occupy the embankment under Lt. Martin, one platoon commanded by Lieut. W.R. Campbell & one by 2nd Lieut. Wishart. Two platoons of the 11th K.R.R.C. also went forward. These two platoons occupied the embankment without any opposition only about two of the enemy were seen on our side trying to get away, one of whom was hit by a piece of shell & was taken prisoner. Orders were received from Division that no posts had to be established	

WAR DIARY or INTELLIGENCE SUMMARY.

Army Form C. 2118.

(Erase heading not required.)

Place	Date	Hour	Summary of Events and Information	Remarks and references to Appendices
	4th to 9th		East of our original line & the two platoons were ordered to withdraw to their normal dispositions. This was carried out in good order. The body of Sgt. Stuart which had been left on the embankment on the 2nd was brought in. No casualties sustained. A patrol which went out later came across the missing section, less one man who had been killed by a sniper, one man drowned whilst trying to cross a broken bridge over the canal & L/Cpl. Blake missing. This section had been cut off owing to the platoons having to withdraw on the afternoon of the 2nd. Active patrolling by day & by night. Enemy put a concentration of mustard & blue cross gas shells near B.H.Q. & D Coy. in reserve. All precautions were taken & there were only a few casualties. A patrol under 2nd Lt. Millar on the night of the 9th came across an enemy post. Bombs were thrown by the enemy who seemed to be much stronger than our patrol but there were no casualties.	
	10th		On the night of the 10/11th a platoon under Lieut. D. Graham went out to try & capture the enemy post located on the night previous. The enemy had apparently moved his post & caught the patrol unexpectedly. Bombs were thrown & Lt. Graham & 8 O.Rs. wounded, 1 killed & 1 missing.	
	11th		A daylight patrol went out on the 11th but could find no trace of the missing or killed men.	
	12 & 13th		Very quiet. Gas was projected by the Special Coy. R.E. on enemy positions opposite the Battalion front on the night of 13/14th. No lights were put up by the enemy.	

WAR DIARY or INTELLIGENCE SUMMARY.

Army Form C. 2118.

(Erase heading not required.)

Place	Date	Hour	Summary of Events and Information	Remarks and references to Appendices
Line	14th & 15th		Very quiet. Usual patrols but enemy seem to be keeping quiet. Bn. relieved by the 11th K.R.R.C. on the 15th. Relief was complete by 9 p.m. Enemy aeroplanes were over. One was caught in the searchlights & dropped his bombs in a hurry one dropping near a platoon of "D" Coy which was marching out.	O.O.
	16th		Baths & cleaning up in LORETTE CAMP.	
	17th & 20th		Training: schemes &c. A long range enemy gun occasionally sends a few shells into ABLAIN during the nights. Officers & N.C.Os. attended a demonstration of a company in attack with tanks.	
	21st & 24th		Training: tactical schemes. A concert in aid of the Pipe Band was very kindly organized by the Division & took place on the 22nd. Concert was a considerable success. On the afternoon of the 23rd Major General Carter Campbell D.S.O. visited the Battalion. The Battalion relieved the 11th Rifle Bde in the AVION SECTION on the night of the 24/25th. D Coy. front line. C. Coy. support. A & B Coy in Reserve.	
	25th – 27th		Patrol were out each night but no enemy encountered. On the night of the 26/27th Operations were carried out by the 8th Div & the 61st Bde. Demonstrations were put up on our front & gas was discharged from our outpost line. There was no hostile retaliation. On the 26th instant Capt. D.P. Knight. (Adj) proceeded on leave.	

WAR DIARY or INTELLIGENCE SUMMARY.

Army Form C. 2118.

Place	Date	Hour	Summary of Events and Information	Remarks and references to Appendices
Line	27th to 30th		During this period active patrolling was carried out by us, as there was an increased expectation of a German withdrawal in the LENS SECTIONS. Our patrols went out to the Rly. embankment at AVION but on each occasion found that it was strongly held. Numerous fires were observed behind the hostile lines during this period.	

T.B.G. Forster Major
for LT. COLONEL,
COMMANDING 2nd Bn: SCOTTISH RIFLES

WAR DIARY
or
INTELLIGENCE SUMMARY.
(Erase heading not required.)

Army Form C. 2118.

2nd Gen. Rif

Place	Date	Hour	Summary of Events and Information	Remarks and references to Appendices
LINE	1st/2nd		Considerable activity in our patrolling as the German withdrawal opposite our front was expected. Daylight patrols were out under 2nd Lt Smith M.C. on the 1st & 2nd instants respectively but on each occasion they were heavily fired on by hostile M.G's on the Rly embankment in AVION. On the night of the third dispositions with the AVION section were changed in view of their expected withdrawal. The Battalion took over part of the front of the 12th Rifle Bde.	
"	3rd		Our patrols were active at dawn & patrol of 2Lt Smith found that the Rly embankment was unoccupied by the enemy. Lt "C" Coy therefore advanced & occupied the embankment with three platoons. Lt D Coy then moved up & pushed forward strong patrols through the line held by C Coy. Their advance was made difficult by heavy M.G fire from the S. end of the BULL RING. They however pushed on rapidly & took SALLAUMINES TR & pushed on to the GREEN LINE (the further side of BULL RING). Their right flank unfortunately was held up by M.G fire from the TRIANGLE & MERICOURT & all movement on their part was heavily fired at. The Battn Hdqrs moved forward to SOURIS TR.	
"	4th		In consequence of the unsatisfactory position of D Coys right flank, it was decided that Lt B. Coy should attack the south end of the BULL RING & the TRIANGLE & clear same of the hostile M.G's. This operation was most successfully carried under Capt D.F. Campbell. Artillery co-operated & B Coy obtained their objectives in the TRIANGLE & MENIAL TR. They captured 2 prisoners of the 164 I.R. 111th DIV. 1 machine Gun, 4 carrier pigeons, numerous rifles, & a considerable quantity of arms & equipment & clothing. The Huns were entirely taken by surprise. Cpl McClelland captured one of the prisoners & Pte. Simpson took the M.G. Lt B Coy then established themselves on the North side of the Triangle & gained touch with Lt. D. Coy	

WAR DIARY or INTELLIGENCE SUMMARY.

(Erase heading not required.)

Army Form C. 2118.

Instructions regarding War Diaries and Intelligence Summaries are contained in F. S. Regs., Part II. and the Staff Manual respectively. Title pages will be prepared in manuscript.

Place	Date	Hour	Summary of Events and Information	Remarks and references to Appendices
LINE.	4th.		Considerable difficulty was found however in gaining touch with the 6th K.S.L.I. on our right who had not advanced at all. This was eventually done on the following day & a liaison post was established W. of MERICOURT. Warning order received stating that the 4th Div. would be relieved by the 12th Div. on or about the 6th. — Lt. Col. Sandilands left the Battn. to go to Staff Course at Camberley.	
	5th.		Our patrols were very active during the day, & touch was eventually gained with the 6th K.S.L.I. — MERICOURT was still held by the enemy, & machine guns & snipers were very active. Rations that night came up as far as the Rly embankment by limbers.	
	6th.		At dawn on this date our artillery was especially active on MERICOURT & it was arranged that after our shelling had ceased that we should send out strong patrols thro' the village. A patrol of the "C" Coy penetrated the village from the west, but were heavily fired on M.G. & snipers. Patrol of B. Coy. under Lt. W. R. Jack moved along the northern outskirts of the village. They reached the N.E corner of the village & were then suddenly fired on from three directions. Their position was very difficult as their only retreat back would be across some 200+ open ground swept of Rifle & M.G fire. They were therefore forced to live out there for the whole day. Many attempts were made to get out to them, & Pte Towers - a runner - eventually found the patrol & brought back information that they intended to	

WAR DIARY or INTELLIGENCE SUMMARY.

Army Form C. 2118.

Place	Date	Hour	Summary of Events and Information	Remarks and references to Appendices
BERLES	6/7th night		withdraw as soon as it became dark. The Towers under heavy fire & under great difficulties managed to return to the Coy. HQrs with the casualty of the patrol. At about 1845 the party got in having suffered casualties 1 killed, 1 missing & 5 wounded. The Battalion was relieved by the 6th Battn. The Buffs, relief being carried out very quietly considering the conditions. After relief platoons marched to FOSSE 6 were there embussed & then proceeded direct to the billets in BERLES. - The same billets as they were in during April.	
	7th		Major T. Foster rejoined the Battn. & assumed command of the Battn. The day was spent in rest & men were left to themselves. - Miniature Range opened in CHATEAU GROUNDS	CHATEAU GROUNDS
	8th		Parades consisted of Inspections of kit etc & generally cleaning up. A & B Coys went to Divisional Baths. - Football Match between A & B Coy v C & D Coys. - B & D Coy winners respectively.	
	9th		Training & Platoon schemes. - B & D Coy. went to Divisional Baths. Final for the best Coy football team resulted in a draw between B & D Coys.	
	10-12		Training in BERLES. - schemes open warfare, village fighting. - D Coy beat B Coy in the Final for Bde Competition	
	13th		Major Foster left the Battn for the Bde wing - Major Gray assumed command.	
	14th		Usual Services. Battalion Route March in the morning - very excellent turn out. Assault training & village fighting.	
	15th		Demonstration of the Battalion in assault formations at different stages of the attack	
	16th		Bn. Route march. The Brigadier General met the Bn. half way & Bn. marched past.	
	17th		Platoon Schemes.	
	18th		Battalion at baths.	
	19th		Schemes. Afternoon :- Battalion Sports came off very successfully. 11th K.R.R.C. kindly lent their band for the occasion. A map showing all the advances this year was put up in the field with the inscription "TO HELL WITH THE BOSCHE : STICK IT THE 90s"	

WAR DIARY
or
INTELLIGENCE SUMMARY.
(Erase heading not required.)

Army Form C. 2118.

Place	Date	Hour	Summary of Events and Information	Remarks and references to Appendices
BERLES	October 20		Divine Service only.	
	21st		Three coys. platoon schemes, one coy. firing on range.	
	22nd to 26th		Platoon schemes with & without troops. All coys. fired on the range.	
	27th		Church parades.	
	28th		Battalion drill under the Commanding Officer. Ceremonial drill.	
	29th		Two coys. A & B fired on the range. C & D coys on an outpost scheme. Orders received about 6 p.m. that the 20th Division will move by tactical train on the 30th inst. to the 3rd Army. Usual work.	
	30th		The Battalion moved from BERLES to CAMBRAI by train & motor lorries. Entrained at SAVY at 6 p.m. & detrained at VELU about 11.30 p.m. Motor lorries were waiting at the detraining station. Kits &c. were unloaded off the train & loaded on the lorries by "D" Coy. in record time. All the men were very happy on the job. "D" Coy. remained at the detraining station to unload all trains of the Brigade group.	O.O.
CAMBRAI	31st		A convoy of 25 motor lorries took the Battalion to CAMBRAI through the devastated area round GOUZEAUCOURT where the Battalion fought during the Boche retreat on the SOMME in 1916. It was a cold ride & owing to breaks in the convoy it was not easy for the O.C. Convoy to keep all his lorries on the right road. Arrived in CAMBRAI at 5 a.m. on the 31st October & all got into fairly comfortable billets. Considering the heavy fighting which took place outside the town it is not too badly knocked about. All the men are in good form & fit.	

P. K. Gray, Major
Commanding 2nd Scottish Rifles

WAR DIARY or INTELLIGENCE SUMMARY

2 Scottish Rfls

Army Form C. 2118.

Vol 48

Place	Date 1918 November	Hour	Summary of Events and Information	Remarks and references to Appendices
CAMBRAI	1st		Cleaning up billets which have been left in a filthy mess by the Bosche.	
	2nd		Baths. Played the 4th Somersets at football.	
CAUROIR	3rd		Battalion marched from CAMBRAI eastwards & billeted for the night in CAUROIR (3 miles). The latter village is not badly wrecked but all the billets are filthy.	00.46
	4th		On the 4th the Battalion marched to St AUBERT (about 9½ miles). Owing to the amount of traffic on the road most of the march was cross country. There was evidence of the the kind of fighting now taking place all the way. There were no systems of trenches; only an isolated bit of trench here & there. No men fell out. There are one or two civilians in St AUBERT who were released when our troops captured the village. There is also every kind of war material left by the Bosche.	00.47
St AUBERT	5th		Rained all day. Men cleaned up billets & collected salvage. Bn. is on two hours notice to move.	
	6th		Still in the same place. Cleaning up all the Bosche filth which he left in billets. (near VENDEGIES about 8 miles)	
SOMMAING	7th		Moved to SOMMAING, & arrived in billets there at 4.30 p.m. Billets are very poor but we are only here for the night.	
	8th		Marched to JENLAIN (about 9 miles), mostly across fields as the roads were very bad. Mud at some parts over the boots. Passed four tanks on the way which had a black cross on them - evidently our tanks being used by the Bosche. There are one or two civilians in JENLAIN who are overjoyed at being released from Bosche rule.	00.48

WAR DIARY or INTELLIGENCE SUMMARY.

Army Form C. 2118.

(Erase heading not required.)

Place	Date	Hour	Summary of Events and Information	Remarks and references to Appendices
	November			
JENLAIN	9th		The whole Battalion is billeted in one farm which is much bigger than most farms in this part of the country. There are about three or four servants who managed to get away from the Bosche starving it. All the horses, cattle & hens were taken away by the Bosche. Bosche has asked for an armistice & his plenipotentiaries have left for our lines. Later news states that he has been given until 11 a.m. on Monday 11th to accept our terms. Bn. is still on half hour's notice to move. One or two bodies of men of English regiments were found in the fields close by. Collected a lot of salvage & cleaned the farm up. The Bosche had left it in the usual mess.	
	10th		Cleaning up billets. Did a little bit of training in the forenoon.	
ST. WAAST	11th		Received orders early to move to ST. WAAST-LA-VALLÉE. Just after breakfast a wire came in stating that the Bosche had accepted our armistice terms & hostilities would cease at 11 a.m. today. This news was at once communicated to the men who made a bit of noise cheering & rattling gas rattles. One or two old soldiers whom one would think had had enough fighting shook their heads & said we should have gone on without an armistice. However everyone seems pleased. Bn. arrived in ST WAAST about 4 p.m. (about 5 miles) & got into billets fairly crowded. Stayed here for the night.	
TAISNIERES	12th		Marched through BAVAY today to TAISNIERES-SUR-HON (about 5 miles) Bn. crowded together in billets which are not too good. But all the houses are whole. The further east we go the less damage has been done	

WAR DIARY or INTELLIGENCE SUMMARY.

Army Form C. 2118.

(Erase heading not required.)

Place	Date	Hour	Summary of Events and Information	Remarks and references to Appendices
TAISNIERES	13th		to the villages. Evidently the Bosche retreat has been a rout in this district. Cleaning up equipment etc. Cleaning up roads & billets in the village. All the civilians are overjoyed at having British soldiers with them again. Many of them last saw Britishers in August 1914. Ours is the first Scotch Battalion most of the people here have seen & quite a stir is created when the pipers turn out to play retreat. They all show their appreciation by clapping their hands. They tell all kinds of stories of the hardships they have suffered at the hands of the Germans.	
	14th		Cleaning up the roads & billets in the village.	
	15th		Had a Battalion parade today & Major Gray read out the terms of the armistice to the Battalion. All the men were delighted with the terms. Afterwards we gave three cheers for the King, for the Army, for the Battalion & for the C.O.	
	16th		Had a Battalion concert at 6 p.m. to which some of the civilians were invited. We played the "Marseillaise" in honour of them. They all said they enjoyed it very much although none of them understood a word that was said.	
	17th		A Thanksgiving service was held in the open. The Brigade was formed up in a hollow square. The weather was against an open air service as it was keen frost so the service had to be cut short.	

WAR DIARY or INTELLIGENCE SUMMARY.

Army Form C. 2118.

Place	Date	Hour	Summary of Events and Information	Remarks and references to Appendices
	November			
TAISNIERES	18th		One company on salvage. Remainder steady drill & cleaning up roads.	
	19th		Under Os. C. Coys. Cleaning up roads.	
	20th		All the Battalion bathed in an old Boche bathing place. Had to have the pioneers working all last night carrying water for the well. Baths were fairly good but the men could get no clean clothing owing to the difficulty of transport, all the railways having been destroyed by the Boche during his retreat.	
	21st		Usual training under Os. C. Coys. Bn. football match against the 62nd Field Ambulance.	
	22nd		Practice Battalion Ceremonial Parade. Could not get a very suitable ground but the men marched past fairly well. We expected to have a Brigade Ceremonial Parade on 23rd but orders came in that we would move on that day.	
WARGNIES-LE-PETIT	23rd		Marched from TAISNIERES to WARGNIES-LE-PETIT (about 8 or 9 miles) The roads were hard with frost & marching was easy. We passed quite a number of released prisoners in BAVAY of all nationalities, all looking very thin.	Q.0.49
BERMERAIN-ST-MARTIN	24th		Marched to BERMERAIN-ST MARTIN (about 8 miles). Roads were still hard. ST MARTIN is fairly well destroyed: not one house in whole.	Q.0.49.
ST VAAST	25th		Marched to ST VAAST (about 8 miles). There has been a thaw & the roads are a bit heavy for marching. Billets are not very good.	

WAR DIARY or INTELLIGENCE SUMMARY.

Army Form C. 2118.

Place	Date November	Hour	Summary of Events and Information	Remarks and references to Appendices
ST VAAST	26th		Expected to move but had orders to stand fast until further orders. Men cleaned up billets & collected salvage.	
CAMBRAI	27th		Started to march to PROVILLE on the Southern outskirts of CAMBRAI. Arrived in CAMBRAI & received orders to halt & await orders. (8 miles) The destination was altered & the Bn. marched into billets in CAMBRAI very near where we were billeted in CAMBRAI about the 30th October. Many civilians have come back to the town since then.	OO.51
	28th		Cleaning up billets & vicinity.	
	29th		Transport moved off this morning en route for the TOUTENCOURT area (West of ALBERT). The Bn. less transport moves by motor lorry on the 30th November.	
TOUTENCOURT	30th		Battalion moved by motor lorries from CAMBRAI to TOUTENCOURT. The route lay through the Somme devastated battlefields via BAPAUME & ALBERT & near places where the Battalion had seen heavy fighting in 1917. Owing to various break downs the convoy was somewhat split up & many men did not arrive in billets until about 8 p.m. having left CAMBRAI at 9 a.m. All the men were billeted in huts in the village & with a little work the huts should be made very comfortable.	OO.52

D.R. Wright Capt & adjt.
for Major
Commanding 2nd Scottish Rifles

WAR DIARY or **INTELLIGENCE SUMMARY**
(Erase heading not required.)

Army Form C. 2118.

2 Scottish Rifles

Instructions regarding War Diaries and Intelligence Summaries are contained in F. S. Regs., Part II. and the Staff Manual respectively. Title pages will be prepared in manuscript.

Place	Date	Hour	Summary of Events and Information	Remarks and references to Appendices
TOUTENCOURT Ref. Map. LENS. 1/100,000	December 1918 1st-3rd		Cleaning up equipment & clothing, repairing the huts where necessary, & sweeping the roads. A great deal of work has to be done in improving the men's huts, making baths, recreation rooms &c. The Education Scheme is starting & training will be partly drill & partly classes under the Education Officer. The Demobilization scheme has also started to work & particulars of employment of every officer & other rank in the Battalion have to be made out.	
	4th		Training under O.s.C. Coys. Mr Harry Dubery lectured to all officers & N.C.Os. of the Brigade on the state of the industries at home & explained how preparations were being made to give employment to the soldiers when they were demobilized.	
	5th		Usual training. Commanding Officer inspected "D" Coy. in marching Order.	
	6th		Inspection of "C" Coy.	
	7th		Usual training & work on huts & baths.	
	8th		Divine Service. The Presbyterian service was taken by the Corps Senior Chaplain. Lecture to officers & N.C.Os. on Demobilization by Colonel HANSING.	

WAR DIARY or INTELLIGENCE SUMMARY.

Army Form C. 2118.

(Erase heading not required.)

Place	Date	Hour	Summary of Events and Information	Remarks and references to Appendices
TOOTENCOURT	December 9th		Training under O.C. Coys. Commanding Officer inspected "A" Coy. Sent 21 men to CAMBRAI for interview with a view to their being sent home as miners. This is the commencement of the Demobilization	
	10th		Usual Training	
	11th		Inspection by the G.O.C. 30th Div was to take place but owing to the rain it had to be cancelled. Baths for the men during the afternoon when change of clothing	
	12th-15th		Usual Parades under O.C. Companies & generally cleaning up of the camps. On Saturday afternoon 14th instant a Battalion Rugby Football team played the R.M.A but were beaten. This was the first time Rugby has been played in the Battalion since 1916. Lieut R.M. Price, our American Medical Officer left the Battalion	
	16th			
	17th-20th		Usual parades during this period. On the 18th the Battalion played the 11th R.B's at Rugby, but were defeated 3-0. On the 19th the Promotion of Major V.R Gray M.C. to Lieut Colonel came through. Eighteen miners went off to CAMBRAI on the 20th — the last batch of miners to go.	
	21st		Parade under O.C. Companies.	
	22nd		"One of the greatest days in the history of the Battalion". At about 10.00 hrs a wire came stating that the VICTORIA CROSS had been awarded to Pte James Towers of B Company for an act of the most unsurpassed bravery performed by him on the 6th Oct this year. The Pipe Band were paraded & played Pte Towers from Battalion Hdqrs through the village to his Billet. He was carried shoulder high by a party of his own platoon & received a great ovation from the whole Battalion.	
	23rd		Battalion parade at 11.00, to practice Ceremonial. — but a heavy downpour of rain rather hampered operations. After the parade the whole Battalion marched past Pte Towers V.C.	

WAR DIARY or INTELLIGENCE SUMMARY.

Army Form C. 2118.

(Erase heading not required.)

Place	Date	Hour	Summary of Events and Information	Remarks and references to Appendices
TOUTENCOURT	24th		Inspection of the Battalion by the Brigade Commander - a very creditable turn out. The general said that it was an excellent show and quite one of the finest ~~battalions~~ that he had seen since he had been in France.	
	25th		Xmas day - no parades. During the morning there was an Inspection of Billets by the CO to determine which was the best decorated hut. Some of the huts were wonderfully decorated and the judging was most difficult. The hut of No 15 Platoon was eventually classed as the winner. All ranks got a good ration of pork & plum pudding with beer for their dinners.	
	26th		Baths during the morning for Companies	
	27th		Usual parades under O.C. Coys. The Battalion paraded in the afternoon outside Hdqrs, and the Brigade Commander presented medal ribbons to the following to some officers & men of the Batt'n, amongst the recipients was Pte Towers V.C.	
	28th		Usual training.	
	29th		Divine Services in the morning	
	30th		Usual parades. Final of the Football Competition for the Bde inter platoon Competition. No 10 Platoon were the victors who will represent the battalion in the Bde Competition.	
	31st		No parades. Sergeants had their New Year dinner to which the Commanding Officer & Officers were invited. The New Year was brought in in good style.	

D.R. Wright Capt. & Adjt.
2nd Scottish Rifles

WAR DIARY or INTELLIGENCE SUMMARY.

Army Form C. 2118.

2 THE SCOTTISH RIFLES

Place	Date 1919	Hour	Summary of Events and Information	Remarks and references to Appendices
TOUTENCOURT	1st January		No parades. New Year dinners for the whole Battalion. The Brigadier went round dinners with the Commanding Officer & wished everyone a Happy New Year.	
	2nd & 3rd		Parades under Os.C. Coys. Filling in trenches & salvageing.	
	4th		All men had to fill in Army Forms for Demobilization purposes.	
	5th		Church parades. Twenty other ranks sent home to be demobilized.	
	6th to 13th		Usual parades. Baths. The Divisional Concert Party commenced giving entertainments in the Brigade Concert Hall at TOUTENCOURT on 7th Jany.	
	14th		Rifle shooting competition. One team per platoon, B.H.Q., Sergeants & officers. Sergeants won. 200 O.Rs. & 3 Officers have been demobelized up to date including Pte. Towers, V.C.	
	15		34 O.R's left Bn for Demobilisation.	
	16		Nothing to report.	
	17		Nothing to report.	
	18		18 other ranks left for Demobilisation.	
	19th		2/Lt J Lang and 16 O.Rs left for Demobilisation	
	20		Major A.S.L. Young Lt. C. BROWNFIELD, and 23 O.R's left for Demobilisation.	

WAR DIARY or INTELLIGENCE SUMMARY

THE SCOTTISH RIFLES

Army Form C. 2118.

Place	Date	Hour	Summary of Events and Information	Remarks and references to Appendices
TOUTENCOURT	Jan 21st		Lt. W.R. MILLIGAN & 22 O.R's left for demobilisation.	
	22nd		Captain D.P. WRIGHT M.C. and 29 O.R's left for demobilisation.	
	23rd		Nothing to report.	
	24th		Nothing to report.	
	25th		Nothing to report.	
	26th		Lt Col Gray was granted 14 days leave to the U.K. A lecture was given to the Bn on Sir Walter Raleigh by Rev. Armstrong. 24 O.R's left for dispersal.	
	27th		2/Lt. N. WISHART & 26 O.R's left the Bn for dispersal.	
	28th		Captain W.O. BRASSINGTON and 17 O.R's left for dispersal. "D" Coy was amalgamated with "C" Coy for messing and discipline & the Command was taken over by Captain D.P. PETRIE D.S.O.	
	29th		20 O.R's left the Bn for dispersal.	
	30th		2/Lieut L.D.C. MCLEES & 34 O.R's left the Bn for dispersal.	
	31st		20 horses in category Y were sent ABBEVILLE with a view to their being shipped to ENGLAND for sale. An interesting lecture by Major FINGAN A.I.F. was given to the Bn. He pointed out the advantages to be gained by going to AUSTRALIA at this time & set forth the Government's scheme for helping ex soldiers of the Imperial Forces.	

WAR DIARY or **INTELLIGENCE SUMMARY.**
(Erase heading not required.)

Army Form C. 2118.

THE SCOTTISH RIFLES.

Place	Date	Hour	Summary of Events and Information	Remarks and references to Appendices
TOUTENCOURT	31st Aug.		During the month the Bn. was kept employed during the morning by filling in trenches, salvaging, wood collecting drill and physical training. In the afternoon football competitions were held. The strength (ration) today is 430.	

D.F. Hemphill. Captain
Comdg. Scottish Rifles

Headquarters
20th Division

Confidential

Herewith War Diary for the month of February.

[signature]
Lieut Colonel
Commanding, 2nd Bn Scottish Rifles

3/3/193

WAR DIARY or INTELLIGENCE SUMMARY.

2 Scottish Rifles

Army Form C. 2118.

THE SCOTTISH RIFLES

Place	Date	Hour	Summary of Events and Information	Remarks and references to Appendices
TOUTENCOURT	FEBY 1st		34 OR's left Bn for dispersal. Captain D.F. PETRIE was granted 10 days leave to PARIS.	
	2nd		Lieuts I.B. McKINLAY & D.H. GALL M.C. & 24 OR's left Bn for dispersal.	
	3rd		Lieut E.H. SMITH & 11 OR's left for dispersal.	
	4th		Orders were received to prepare for the move at short notice of 10 officers and 300 OR's to ROUEN to join the 1st Cameronians. The men were to be selected in accordance with A.O. 14. which provided for retention of men in the Service who had not enlisted prior to Jan. 1st 1916	
	5th		Nothing to report.	
	6		19 other ranks left Bn for dispersal.	
	7th		Lieut T. DAWSON and 3 other ranks left Bn for dispersal	
	8th		19 other ranks left Bn for dispersal	
	9th		2/Lieut D. HAMILTON and 23 other ranks left Bn for dispersal	
	10th		14 other ranks left Bn for dispersal. 2/Lt H. HENDERSON admitted to hospital.	
	11th		The C.O. inspected draft of men to be retained in the service, about to proceed to ROUEN in marching order. The turnout was very good.	

WAR DIARY or INTELLIGENCE SUMMARY.

(Erase heading not required.)

Army Form C. 2118.

THE SCOTTISH RIFLES

Place	Date	Hour	Summary of Events and Information	Remarks and references to Appendices
TOUTENCOURT.	12th		A draft composed as follows left Bn to join 1st Bn The Cameronians at ROUEN. They were conveyed in Motor Lorries to DOULLENS. Capt D.P. PETRIE D.S.O. Commanding. Lts. J.L. CUNNINGHAM, W.R. CAMPBELL, R. GRANT, 2/Lieuts W.B. JACK M.C. and J.B. WEBSTER. Other ranks 132.	
	13th		15 other ranks left Bn for disposal. Strength of Bn today is 5 officers and 153 other ranks.	
	14th		3 other ranks left the Bn for disposal.	
	15th		2/Lieut G. SMITH was granted 2 months leave.	
	16th		11 other ranks left the Bn for disposal.	
	17		Nothing to report.	
RAINCHEVAL.	18th		The Bn. marched to RAINCHEVAL 5 kilometres N.W. of TOUTENCOURT.	
"	19th		Nothing to report.	
"	20		Nothing to report.	
"	21		2/Lt HENDERSON left and 14 O.Rs left Bn for disposal.	
"	23rd		R.S.M. A. SMART promoted to 2 Qr. in today's London Gazette.	
	28th		Draft of 55 other ranks including 2 C.S.M's left Bn for disposal & was inspected by the Brigade Commander. 10 horses were also sent away for sale to the BELGIANS	

V.B. Gray
Lt.-Col.
Comdg 2/Sco Rifles.

1. S.A.S.
3rd Echelon.

Received War Diary for the
month of March.

[signature]
Lieut. Col.
Cmdg. Vector Rifles.

FRANCE
3.4.19

CONFIDENTIAL.

WAR DIARY or INTELLIGENCE SUMMARY

Army Form C. 2118.

THE SCOTTISH RIFLES
Vol 52

Place	Date March	Hour	Summary of Events and Information	Remarks and references to Appendices
RAINCHEVAL	1		Summer time came into force to-day.	
	2ⁿᵈ		Nothing to report.	
	3ʳᵈ 5ᵗʰ 6ᵗʰ		3 favourite horses were sent to the Base for transfer to ENGLAND.	
	7ᵗʰ		Lt. A. LAWSON and S. MACFARLANE and 9 O.R's left Bn for dispersal on leave. Draft was inspected by G.O.C. Division.	
	8ᵗʰ		G.O.C. Divn. inspected the cadre in Marching Order, and afterwards Mob. Stores.	
TERRAMESNIL	10ᵗʰ		Bn moved to TERRAMESNIL. 5 kilometres N.W. of RAINCHEVAL. 11ᵗʰ 60ᵗʰ & 11ᵗʰ R.B. assisted in the move by lending 5 pair horses.	
	11ᵗʰ		3 L.D. horses were sent away.	
	12ᵗʰ		Nothing to report.	
	13		Verbal orders were received to be prepared to proceed to the U.K. on 17ᵗʰ inst. New Demobilisation Tables were taken into use.	
	14		Move of cadre on 17ᵗʰ was postponed.	
	15		One half of Regt Transport was moved to Divnl. Transport Park MONDICOURT accompanied by a guard of 2 NCO. & 6 men.	
	16		Remainder of transport except 2 G.S. wagons 1 water cart & 1 Mess cart was sent to MONDICOURT. All the Mobilisation stores were packed in the wagons. Unserviceable stores were inspected & condemned by an Ordnance Board.	
	17		All the animals with the exception of 4 L.D. horses and 5 mules have been transferred to other units.	

WAR DIARY
or
INTELLIGENCE SUMMARY.
(Erase heading not required.)

Army Form C. 2118.

THE SCOTTISH RIFLES.

Place	Date	Hour	Summary of Events and Information	Remarks and references to Appendices
TERRAMESNIL	Nov 1	18th	Nothing to report.	
"		19th	"	
"		20th	"	
"		21st	"	
		22nd	The officers of the cadre paid a visit to parts of the devastated area over which the 90th had fought including OVILLERS LA BOISELLE, LES BOEUFS, ST PIERRE VAAST Wood, and MORLAINS. Near the site of ZENITH Trench which was captured by the Bn on 23rd Oct 1916 several scattered graves were found; amongst these, were those of D. Stewart and 2 "unknown officers" of the Bn. Orders were received for the cadre to entrain at MONDICOURT on 25th inst to proceed to ENGLAND but were cancelled the same day owing to the possibility of a strike by miners, transport workers, and NUR	ZENITH Trench ½ mile N.E. of LES BOEUFS
		23rd	Nothing to report.	
		24th	Normal movement of cadres to ENGLAND was resumed, & the cadre was held in readiness to proceed next day.	
		25th	The movement of cadre was cancelled until further orders	
		26th	Nothing to report.	
		27th	4 L.D. Horses were dispatched to Corps Animal Collecting Camp.	
		28th	6 other ranks left Bn. for 2 months leave prior to Foreign Service. Orders for cadre to entrain at CANDAS on 30th inst to proceed to ENGLAND were received.	

WAR DIARY or INTELLIGENCE SUMMARY

Army Form C. 2118.

(Erase heading not required.)

Place	Date	Hour	Summary of Events and Information	Remarks and references to Appendices
TERRAMESNIL	29.		All Regtl. Transport previously parked at MONDICOURT was taken to CANDAS under Divisional arrangement.	
"	30th		Cadre moved to CANDAS by motor lorry. Wagons were loaded on 11 flats; 1/3 railway coach was allotted to the officers, 2 coves to the men and 1 cover for stores. Train left CANDAS at 15.30 hrs.	
HAVRE.	31st		Train arrived at HAVRE about 05.00 hours, but did not reach Entraining station till 12.00 hours. After the wagons were off loaded they were taken to the docks by the R.A.S.C. The cadre marched to No.1 Reception Camp.	

V.M.Gray.
Lieut-Col.
Comdg. 2/Cartier Rifles.

Confidential.

O.U.Y.
3rd October
FRANCE

2/3
4/
93

Herewith War Diary from
1st to 8th April inclusive.

13

(Signature)
Commdg. 2/Scottish Rifles

WAR DIARY or INTELLIGENCE SUMMARY.

Army Form C. 2118.

THE SCOTTISH RIFLES

Place	Date April	Hour	Summary of Events and Information	Remarks and references to Appendices
HAVRE	1st		Cadre left No 1 Reception Camp & passed through a delousing camp where every man had a bath & was given clean under clothing. All the remainder of their kit was deloused. From here it proceeded to No 1 Dispatch Camp to await sailing orders.	
	2nd		Nothing to report	
	3rd		Nothing to report	
	4th		Nothing to report	
	5th		All transport & mobilisation stores were loaded on S.S. HUNTSCLYDE. Loading was carried out by Royal Marines.	
	6th		Cadre embarked on S.S. TURBINIA. Left HAVRE 18.00 hours arrived SOUTHAMPTON 02.30 hours 7th	
	7th		Cadre off loaded transport & loaded it on a special train which left SOUTHAMPTON at 16.40 hours.	
	8th		Cadre arrived in COLCHESTER at 01.30 hours. took over GOOJERAT Barracks.	

www.ingramcontent.com/pod-product-compliance
Lightning Source LLC
Chambersburg PA
CBHW081123817042G
43191CB00034B/1970

9 781474 511773